C000201117

for
LOVE, ROMANCE &
MARRIAGE

Feng shui in small doses for
Love, Romance & Marriage.
by
Lillian Too
© Konsep Lagenda S/B

ISBN 983 - 9778 - 10 - 2

Also in this series

Wealth and Prosperity

Work and Career

Published by
KONSEP BOOKS
Malaysia
April 2000

For Love, Romance & Marriage

1

For love to flourish in your life create the essence of good affinity feng shui in your home.

Do this by protecting and activating the SOUTHWEST, the universal corner for romance

2

Use a good compass to mark out the Southwest corner. Then energize both the BIG CHI SOUTHWEST (ie of the whole house) as well as small chi southwest - of each room separately.

3

Light up your love life
with bright lights.
When the SW corners of
your home are well
lighted, it attracts the
energy of romance luck.
Use white, red
or yellow lights.

4

Place a cluster of natural quartz crystals to simulate the element of earth. Crystals carry the excellent chi of the earth. Place it on a table in the SW corner.

5

If there is a toilet in your Southwest corner, your love luck becomes seriously afflicted. Hang a five-rod windchime above the toilet OR paint the inside of the door a bright red OR hang a large mirror on the outside of the door.

For Love, Romance & Marriage

6

If your SW corner is missing, activate its chi by focusing on the SW of your living or dining room. This creates the small chi, which is just as powerful as the BIG CHI of the whole house.

7

In feng shui, romance,
love and marriage are
all part of family luck.

Life is considered
incomplete when family
luck is missing.

8

Feng shui can enhance
romance in your life
and bring you a life
partner but it is not for
the frivolous.

Unless you are ready
for a commitment don't
energize for love.

9

Activating love feng shui brings marriage opportunities and causes marriage luck to ripen. But it does not guarantee a perfect match. That depends on your karma

For Love, Romance & Marriage

10

Feng shui is earth luck.
It accounts for one third
of your overall luck.

The quality of your love
relationships depends
on your heaven and
mankind luck.

11

The universal love
corner is always the
Southwest and this is
the place of the <u>kun</u>
trigram which
symbolizes the chi of
the matriarch.
This corner brings big
earth luck.

12

If you have heavy
exposed overhead
beams in the SW,
camouflage the edges
of these beams with
patterns or hang tiny
windchimes that soften
the killing chi of the
edges.

13

The Southwest is of the earth element. The presence of flowers and plants deplete the energy of earth. So never put plants in the Southwest if you want your marriage luck to flourish

14

Decorative objects placed in the Southwest should never be made of wood. Nor should there be fresh flowers in the SW. Instead decorate with porcelain, clay or crystal objects.

15

Water in the Southwest
is also very harmful,
since the elements of
earth and water are
not harmonious. Water
here afflicts relationship
luck and cause
residents to quarrel all
the time.

16

Decorative urns, ceramics and crystal chandeliers are excellent for activating romance luck when placed in the SW. Get those that are painted with auspicious objects for extra luck.

17

An excellent energizer for the SW corner is the heart shaped quartz crystal. Place it on a table preferably resting on a red tablecloth or on any red base to bring love luck.

18

Natural quartz crystal and jasper are powerful natural energizers in both the earth corners of the home. In the SW it activates romance luck and in the NE it brings literary luck.

19

The Kun trigram of the SW can also be activated by incorporating three yin broken lines onto furniture, ceiling designs, cornices and walls. Kun activates marriage luck.

20

Hang a painting of high mountains in the SW corner of the house.

This creates the powerful chi of big earth, which ensures harmony and goodwill in all your relationships

21

If you have a
protruding corner in
any of your SW corners,
do not use plants or
windchimes as a
remedy. Better to shine
a bright light directly at
the edges to dissolve
the bad energy.

22

When the SW corners of
the home are afflicted
the relationships in your
life will suffer.

It can even cause
spouses to separate,
sometimes permanently.

23

When the SW corner of the home is missing due to its shape, marriage and relationships tend to lack depth and be superficial.

Place a BIG boulder or crystal to compensate.

24

Missing SW corners also cause a serious lack in your social life. Best solution is to install a bright light to shine directly at the wall. This will symbolically create chi energy for the corner.

25

Placing a large mirror on one wall of a SW sector creates "virtual space" inside the mirror. Correct a missing SW corner this way only if it is not the bedroom, the kitchen or a toilet.

26

Mirrors in any part of the home must never reflect a door, a staircase, a toilet or a kitchen. Mirrors must reflect auspicious objects. Reflection of earth objects bring romance luck.

27

To jump start romance luck in your life, try painting one wall of the SW a bright red. This creates precious yang energy. Yellow and white are good alternatives, but red is best!

28

A crystal chandelier in the Southwest is one of the best methods of energizing this universal love corner.

Keep the light switched on for at least 3 hours each night.

29

If you cannot afford a chandelier, get a lampshade that is bright red for the SW.

Write auspicious words on the lampshade and keep the light turned on for three hours.

30

Hang a faceted crystal
ball, about one inch in
diameter, on a window
in the SW corner.

This captures afternoon
sunlight turning them
into chi-laden rainbows.
Most auspicious.

31

Floating candles placed in a bowl laden with crystals, glass beads or semi precious stones also activate the SW.

Use three candles. Never use two candles as this signifies death.

32

Don't go overboard
energizing the SW.
When you overdo the
feng shui, you might
create imbalance. So
choose one tip which
appeals to you, and
implement it.
Use one tip at a time.

33

How do you find out the SW corner of the house? You must use a good compass. Stand in the center of the house or in the center of the room and take your bearings carefully. Any other way is incorrect

34

Balance the yang chi of the masculine with the yin chi of the feminine - let both types of chi permeate the energies of your home, and especially the bedroom.

35

Paintings, colour schemes and decorative objects must never be excessively masculine or feminine if you want romance and marriage luck to rise and grow.

Have a bit of both.

36

Yin and yang
harmoniously balanced,
create relationship chi -
a 'pairing of opposites',
sunlight with moonlight;
water with mountains;
male with female.

Romance!

37

Mix warm and cool colours when you decorate. Paint living and dining areas with bright yang colours and drench bedrooms with dark restful yin hues. This balances the chi correctly.

38

An excellent symbol of endless love is the mystic knot also known as the love knot. Stick red love knots on pictures of you and your partner to create smooth love chi between you.

39

When sending flowers to your sweetheart, don't send flowers with thorns. Red roses may be romantic (and they are) but get rid of the spikes if you don't want the relationship to end.

40

The most auspicious colour for flowers - which encourage romance to blossom seriously are yellow flowers. This is bright yang and it signifies the vital energy of mother earth.

41

Never send white flowers for love. While they may be great for older people they do nothing for those who are young and in love. White flowers should be reserved for mature people

42

Display a pair of
mandarin ducks in
your bedroom.

This symbolizes the
happiness of lovers. If
you are single this
creates healthy love chi
to attract a partner

43

Mandarin ducks are
best when made of
crystal or jasper
although colourful
wooden ones are also
good especially if your
personalized romance
corner is east or
southeast

44

Never display mandarin ducks singly. This suggests you will stay single forever. And don't display them in threes either as this implies infidelity.

Two is the only correct number.

45

If your long time boyfriend or girlfriend refuses to commit consider investing in a screen with a pair of flying geese for his/her bedroom. These are symbols of eternal love and symbolize marriage destinies.

For Love, Romance & Marriage

46

Geese should always be displayed as a pair.

It is best to show them flying together because this represents a happy marriage where there is the happy togetherness of mutual interests.

47

If you are single and live alone, you will benefit from strong earth energy as this creates the chi of family luck.

Place boulders, crystals or a mountain picture in your living room.

48

Also stimulate earth
energy with a sculpture
that has a stone base
like marble or clay.
Place something of this
material in the foyer
area flanking the door
to welcome in the
earth energy.

49

Women who wish to attract potential husbands should ensure there is plenty of male yang energy in the home. Do not allow your home décor to get excessively feminine.

50

Single men who wish to
settle down should
activate their SW and
introduce strong
feminine chi into
their homes. Hang
paintings of the moon,
or of women. Avoid
excessively yang
energy.

51

At all times maintain
harmonious balance in
the home. Sun and
moon symbols
complement each other,
as do dark and light,
sunshine and shade.
Maintain a good mix of
yin with yang.

52

Water features in the wrong corners can lead to sex scandals, infidelity and difficult relationships. Water should never be on the right side of the main door. (inside looking out)

53

Never place a water
feature in the bedroom.
Aquariums, moving
water bowls and even
paintings with water
scenes should be kept
out of the bedroom.
They cause loss.

54

Water to the right of the main door either inside or outside the house cause the husband to develop a roving eye and get entangled in a relationship outside the marriage.

55

Be careful of swimming pools. Large bodies of water can 'drown' relationships causing unhappiness & separations. In severe cases such feng shui affliction can even lead to divorce.

56

Avoid putting cactus
and plants with thorns
in the SW. The negative
impact on your love
luck gets magnified and
relationships will reflect
the prickly attributes of
these plants.

57

Never give loved ones gifts that are prickly, sharp or have cutting edges. Don't buy letter openers, scissors or cactus plants as gifts. They cause romance to fizzle out pretty fast.

58

If you have a garden, install a bright globe light five feet above the ground. This draws vital earth energy from the ground thereby activating romance and marriage chi.

59

If your kitchen is in the SW of your home it presses down on your love luck but if your stove is in the SW corner of the kitchen it nullifies the bad effect. Fire strengthens earth.

60

Young unmarried
bachelors and girls
benefit from hanging
images of the peony in
their bedrooms.

Peonies symbolize a
happy love life and
bring marriage luck.

61

When all the children have married, remove peony images and paintings from the bedroom. Otherwise the patriarch's libido cause him to lose his head to a sweet young thing.

62

It is a bad idea to have fresh flowers in the bedroom of a married couple. This can cause either of them to look for love elsewhere outside the marriage. Dried flowers are worse.

63

Mirrors that directly
reflect the bed can
cause the marriage of
the sleeping residents to
become crowded.
Outside third parties
cause problems,
infidelities and even,
heartbreak.

64

Married couples should not sleep on two separate single-bed mattresses that are placed on a double bed frame. This creates an invisible barrier between the couple.

65

Either sleep on a proper double bed with a double bed mattress or sleep on two separate single beds placed side by side. The feng shui is not harmed if beds face different directions.

66

An exposed overhead beam 'cutting' the sleeping couple below harms them. When cut horizontally across the bodies it hurts their love life. When it cuts vertically it causes them to separate.

67

Couples should never sleep with their feet pointed to the door. This simulates the 'death' position, and one of them could end up losing the other. Move the bed to one side.

68

Placing a crystal heart
in the bedroom will
enhance feelings of love
between the couple.
Place the heart on the
night table inside a
velvet pouch or place it
under the pillow.

69

Energize your crystal
with yang energy by
bathing it in sunlight.
Place it in the sun for
three hours over seven
consecutive days.
Morning sun is softer
and finer than
excessively hot
afternoon sun.

70

Magnify the love chi of
the crystal heart with
precious moon energy
over a fifteen-day cycle
of the moon. On the
night of the full moon is
when the moon
energies are strongest.

71

The double happiness
symbol is a powerfully
potent emblem of
conjugal bliss. Wear a
double happiness ring
to celebrate your
marriage or
engagement. This is
feng shui you can wear!

For Love, Romance & Marriage

72

Decorate with the double happiness symbol in the master bedroom - stick it on furniture, walls, curtains and sheets if you wish. But remember not to overdo it. Stay balanced.

73

The double happiness
sign is especially
meaningful when
combined with lights
and lanterns. Paint it on
red lampshades to light
up good marriage feng
shui in the bedroom.

74

Use the powerfully potent EIGHT MANSIONS FORMULA to determine your personal love corner that is most auspicious for you according to your date of birth and gender. Learn to calculate your KUA number.

75

KUA numbers are based on the Chinese calendar year of birth. Those born before Feb 4th must deduct one year off their year of birth to work out their KUA numbers

76

Add the last two digits
of your year of birth.
Keep adding until a
single digit. For males
deduct this number
from 10. The result is
your KUA number. For
females add 5 to this
number.

77

The table shows your romance direction.

Your KUA #	Romance direction
1	South
2	Northwest
3	Southeast
4	East
5 male	Northwest
5 female	West
6	Southwest
7	Northeast
8	West
9	North.

78

Use your personal
romance direction to
energize marriage luck.
Sleep with your head
pointed to this direction.
When you lie
horizontally your head
should be pointing
towards this direction.

79

When on a date, try to sit facing your personal romance direction, especially when you are eating a meal and engaged in chatting up someone you like.

80

Try to sleep in the room
that is located in your
personal love corner of
the house. If your love
direction is north,
choose a bedroom that
is located in the north
part of your home.

81

In feng shui terms your personal love direction is called your *nien yen* direction. Magnifying the energies of your nien yen will activate lucky family and marriage luck for you.

82

If your nien yen is south, you should activate the chi of the fire element. Do this by placing a bright light in this corner of the living room. This will attract romantic opportunities.

83

If your nien yen is north, activate with blue and place a moon sign there. Do not energize the north with water as this could lead to complications in love affairs. Water is better for wealth than for love.

84

If your nien yen is east
or southeast, activate
these corners with
flowers - use the peony
or the plum blossom
which symbolize
happiness in love and
marriage.

85

If your nien yen is west or northwest, use bells to create the relationship luck of these metal element corners. Bells are preferred to windchimes for activating the luck of romance.

86

If your nien yen is
southwest or northeast,
energizing these corners
have a doubly potent
effect. This is because
love and relationships
are associated with
earth. Display crystals.

87

The key to fast results to using the nien yen direction is to ensure that your sleeping position and sitting direction always taps into it. Nien yen brings marriage and family.

88

Flying star principles can bring powerful romance luck into your life in a remarkably short time. The flying star natal chart can identify the most auspicious corner for romance in any home.

89

There are 24 possible house natal charts for every period. We are in period 7 which ends in 2004. Natal charts are determined according to date of house construction and main door orientation.

90

Recommendations given here are for Period 7 homes built between 1984 to 2004. Door orientations produce the natal chart, which indicates the corner of the house or rooms that offer romance luck.

91

Homes with main doors that face South 1 (between 157.5 to 172.5 degrees) must activate the Northwest with a crystal or boulders for romance luck. East corners benefit from a water feature.

92

Where main door faces South 2/3 (between 172.5 to 202.5 degrees) the southeast is the auspicious romance corner. Activate with still water and grow some water plants like lotus.

93

If main door is facing North 1 (between 337.5 to 352.5 degrees) the corner most auspicious for love is the East corner. Use still water and water plants to enhance this corner.

94

If main door is facing North 2/3 (between 352.5 to 022.5 degrees) the West corner is very lucky for romance luck. You are advised to energize this West corner with a 7-rod windchime.

95

Where main door is facing West 1 (between 247.5 to 262.5 degrees) romance luck is in the southeast but it has to be strongly activated with fire. The wood element here needs fire chi (warmth) to flower.

96

If the main door is
facing West 2/3
(between 262.5 to 292
degrees) romance luck is
in the Northwest.

Energize with a 6 rod
windchime or with a
cluster of crystals.

97

If your main door faces East 1 (between 067.5 to 082.5 degrees) romance is governed by the luck of the south sector.

Place big boulders in the South to attract romance luck.

98

If your main door faces
East 2/3 (between 082.5
to 112.5 degrees) you
have to place boulders
in the North corner.
A water feature should
be small and still, or it
could affect your
marriage.

99

When the main door is facing Southwest 1 (between 202.5 to 217.5 degrees) romance luck resides in Northeast. Enhance this sector with crystals, boulders or a bright red lamp.

100

Main door facing Southwest 2/3 (between 217.5 to 247.5 degrees) have romance luck, concentrated in the Southwest part of the house near the entrance. Strengthen with crystals and lights.

101

Main door facing Southeast 1 (between 112.5 to 127.5 degrees) romance and marriage luck is lacking. Strengthen the relationship star in the South sector with crystals.

102

Homes with main door
facing Southeast 2/3
(between 127.5 to 157.5
degrees) must activate
the relationship star in
the North with crystals
to attract some
romance luck.

103

Main door facing Northeast 1 (between 022.5 to 037.5 degrees) have excellent love luck. Strengthen further with crystals placed in the center of the home and with anything metallic placed in the Northeast.

104

Homes with the main door facing Northeast 2/3 (between 037.5 to 067.5 degrees) also have excellent love luck. Strengthen with crystals in the center of the home and in the Southwest.

105

Homes with the main
door facing Northwest
1 (between 292.5 to
307.5 degrees) must
activate with boulders
tied with red thread in
West corners to protect
the women's marriage
and family luck.

106

Homes with the main door facing Northwest 2/3 (between 307.5 to 337.5 degrees) should protect the women of the household with strong earth energy in the east. Must not activate the SW.

107

If you are activating romance luck with water use very small water features like aquariums. Too much moving water indicates a good start to romance but a sad ending.

108

Release a helium filled love balloon. Write down the name of the one you love and send your secret wishes into the Cosmos. Romance may yet blossom between the two of you.

109

Paste dragon and phoenix symbols in your bedroom to simulate this auspicious celestial pairing. Excellent for older bachelors and spinsters looking for marriage opportunities.

110

Light three red candles each day for the fifteen days of the Chinese New Year to ensure happy marriage luck throughout the year. Those still single will meet eligible potential partners.

111

Display plenty of plum blossoms and chrysanthemums during the fifteen days of the Chinese New Year to attract romance luck during the course of the coming year. Ladies should wear red.

112

If you want to catch a good husband, throw one ripe and succulent orange into the sea or river on the fifteenth night of the New Year celebrations. This is an auspicious full moon night.

113

You can also blow bubbles filled with all your romantic wishes on any night of the full moon. Invoke the blessings of the God of marriage who is said to reside in the moon.

114

Write your most fervent
romantic wish and sign
it 49 times, then burn it.
Do this everyday for a
total period of 49 days.
I am told that this 49
day signing ritual
brings you your wish.

115

Protect your love luck from the deadly five yellow annual flying star. Each year find out where it resides in your home and hang a 5 rod windchime there to keep it under control.

116

The deadly five yellow is
in the NORTH in 2000;
in the Southwest in 200,
in the EAST in 2002
and in the SOUTHEAST
IN 2003.
Don't let the 5 yellow
spoil your love life.

117

People with KUA numbers 1,3,4 and 9 belong to East group; those with KUA 2,5,6,7, and 8 are West group. Generally people from the same group are more compatible with each other.

118

Chinese astrology 12 animal types are classified into groups of three known as affinity triangles. People who belong to the same triangle are said to be extremely well matched.

119

THE COMPETITIVE TYPES
are the rat, monkey and
dragon.
THE INDEPENDENT SPIRITED
are the horse, dog and tiger

THE INTELLECTUALS are the
snake, rooster and the ox

THE DIPLOMATS are the
sheep, rabbit and boar.

120

Arrows of antagonism exist between those born exactly six years apart. These people are completely incompatible and marriage between them is best avoided. Don't even start a romance!

121

Incompatible animals of the Chinese Zodiac: Boars clash with the Snake. Rats clash with the Horse. Ox clash with the Sheep. Tigers clash with the Monkey. Rabbits clash with the Rooster. Dragons clash with the Dog

122

Earth types make excellent husbands. These are guys born in the years of the Dog, the Ox, the Dragon and the Sheep. Irrespective of compatibility these earth types will be protective.

123

The seductive women of the Chinese Zodiac are the Snake (fire); the Rabbit (wood) and the Sheep (earth). If you're up against any of these three for a man, they will have the upper hand.

124

Overcome the Snake
with water. Wear black.

Overcome the Sheep
with wood. Wear green.

Overcome the Rabbit
with metal (wear gold)

125

For protection women should always carry a mirror when they go clubbing or to singles bars. Use it to reflect the whole place once over at the start of the evening to dissolve any bad energy.

126

Another excellent
symbol of protection
against unwanted
advances is the fan.
Single women should
carry a small fan to
symbolically ward off
bad intentions.

127

When you are single, always wear something red on your body to simulate the presence of yang energy. This attracts marriage and family luck, but too much yang can kill romance

128

When you have happily married, guard against third party intrusion into your idyll by banning mirrors from the bedroom and water features from the right of your main door.

Dedication

*for my family
with love*

FENG SHUI
on line at

www.worldoffengshui.com

www.lillian-too.com

www.lilliantoojewellery.com

EMAIL the author at
Feng shui@ lillian-too.com